Spring

Adult Coloring book

LARGE PRINT

Copyrights: Ginny Rose
ISBN:9798385936984

THIS BOOK BELONGS TO:

TEST COLOR PAGE

Thank you for purchasing this coloring book. We know it will be time well spent for you!

You're about to start filling 60 beautiful spring-themed coloring pages with color!

Have fun!

Check out the **"Four Seasons"** coloring book series, in which you will find a coloring book for every season!

Check out **your next favorite** coloring book for summer!

Source files used in book: Canva

Made in United States
Cleveland, OH
26 June 2025

17994792R00072